VOLCANO, EARTHQUAKE ~ AND ~ HURRICANE

Nick Arnold

Wayland

Dangerous Waters

MONSTERS OF THE DEEP
PIRATES AND TREASURE
VOYAGES OF EXPLORATION
THE WHALERS

Frontiers

GREAT JOURNEYS
MAPPING THE UNKNOWN
THE WILD, WILD WEST
THE WORLD'S WILD PLACES

Fearsome Creatures

BIRDS OF PREY
LAND PREDATORS
NIGHT CREATURES
WHEN DINOSAURS RULED THE
EARTH

The Earth's Secrets

FOSSILS AND BONES
THE HIDDEN PAST
THE SEARCH FOR RICHES
VOLCANO, EARTHQUAKE AND
HURRICANE

Produced for Wayland (Publishers) Limited by
Roger Coote Publishing
Gissing's Farm, Fressingfield, Eye
Suffolk IP21 5SH, England

Series designer: Jane Hannath
Book designer: Victoria Webb
Editor: Katie Roden

First published in 1996 by
Wayland (Publishers) Limited, 61 Western Road
Hove, East Sussex BN3 1JD, England

British Library Cataloguing in Publication Data

Arnold, Nick
    Volcano, Earthquake and Hurricane. – (Quest)
    1. Volcanoes – Juvenile literature 2. Earthquakes –
    Juvenile literature 3. Hurricanes – Juvenile literature
    4. Natural disasters – Juvenile literature
    I. Title
    363.3'49

    ISBN 0 7502 1386 8

Printed and bound in Italy by
G. Canale & C.S.p.A., Turin

Picture acknowledgements
Camera Press *front cover* bottom left, 5b/N Blickov, 7l,
14-15/Jaccard, 19/Rosenquist/Earth, 23b/ERMA, 25/ERMA,
27b/ERMA, 39b/Vanya Kewley, 42/Anwar Hossain; CM
Dixon 4b; Mary Evans Picture Library 7t, 18b, 39t, 41b;
Geoscience Features 4l, 11r, 12t, 12-13, 34; Robert
Harding Picture Library *front cover* right/Douglas Peebles,
20, 28-9/Adrian Neville; Hulton Deutsch 8 both, 10-11,
17t, 28t, 33t; Image Select 16b, 23l; Impact 22/Paul
Forster, 24t/Philip Gordon, 27r/Peter Menzel; Frank Lane
Picture Agency *front cover* centre left/W Carlson,
9t/Tomas Kicek, 21t/USDA, 37t/NASA, 38t/Australian
Information Service, 41t/W Carlson; Peter Newark's
Pictures 6, 33b, 35b; Oxford Scientific Films 17c/Dieter
and Mary Plage/Survival, 26t/Warren Faidley, 35r/Warren
Faidley, 36b/Warren Faidley; Rex Features 13t/SIPA,
14/Carraro, 15t, 31, 40/SIPA/Voja Miladinovic, 42-
3/SIPA/Voja Miladinovic; Science Photo Library 44; Tony
Stone Images 9b/G Brad Lewis, 45/Ken Biggs; Zefa 1,
10b/K Kerth, 30b/Ned Gillette. The artwork is by Peter
Bull 16l, 18t, 28b, 30r, 37l, 41c; and Tony Townsend 5t,
7b, 17b, 21b, 24b, 26l, 32, 36t.

CONTENTS

WHAT CAUSES NATURAL DISASTERS?

PLANET Earth is a dangerous place. Only about 30 km beneath your feet it is hot enough to melt rock as if it were ice-cream. In some places, this molten rock, or magma, forces its way to the surface to produce a volcano. Sometimes a

Left When a volcano erupts red-hot ash and rocks are thrown high into the air.

Below This dog was buried by ash in the erup-tion of Vesuvius. The chain around its neck prevented it from escaping.

Terrified and homeless

The ancient Roman writer Pliny the Younger wrote an account of a volcanic eruption that destroyed the city of Pompeii in Italy in AD 79. Here he describes the plight of the survivors: 'People bewailed their own fate or that of their relatives, and there were some that prayed for death in their terror of dying. Many asked the help of the gods, but still more imagined there were no gods left, and that the universe was plunged into eternal dark-ness for evermore.'

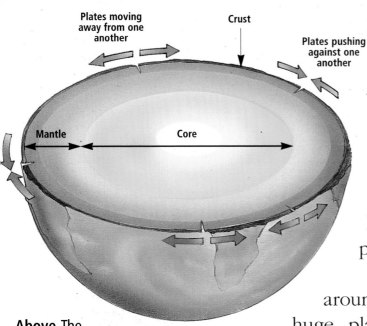

Plates moving away from one another

Crust

Plates pushing against one another

Mantle

Core

Above The three main layers of the Earth. In the central core, the temperature is 2,500 °C. The 2,900-km thick mantle is mainly solid rock, except nearest the surface where it is molten. The outer layer, the crust, varies from 5 to 50 km thick. The plates that make up the crust float on the molten mantle and are moved around by huge, slow-moving currents within it.

volcano explodes in a blast more powerful than the most destructive bomb ever invented, and when this happens thousands of people can lose their lives.

The thin surface layer around the Earth is made up of huge plates of rock which are constantly on the move. As they grind and jolt against one another, they cause earthquakes that can destroy an entire city in minutes. They can also produce giant sea waves called tsunami, which can drown tens of thousands of helpless victims.

Added to these are the threats of hurricanes and tornadoes – powerful, whirling storms with winds of up to 300 km/h that can destroy almost everything in their path. Hurricanes also bring storm surges that can flood low-lying coastal areas.

Below In 1988, a terrible earthquake in Armenia killed 50,000 people. The picture shows soldiers and other rescuers searching for survivors in the ruins of a building.

5

WHAT HAPPENS WHEN A VOLCANO ERUPTS?

O N 24 August AD 79, the citizens of Pompeii in Italy awoke to a beautiful, cloudless morning. Crowds gathered in the public square to celebrate a religious festival. Earth tremors had been shaking the town for several days, but none of Pompeii's 8,000 citizens had blamed them on the tranquil peak of Mount Vesuvius, 10 km to the northwest. The mountain had been quiet for eight centuries.

The home of a wealthy citizen of Pompeii at the time of the eruption of Vesuvius in AD 79. The rooms are beautifully painted and on the floor there are mosaics made from thousands of tiny coloured stones.

The ash from the volcano has preserved the shape of this victim's body.

A Roman soldier shelters from the torrent of ash and volcanic rock.

At about noon, as people went about their everyday business, Vesuvius erupted with a resounding crash, like a vast door slamming. The ground shook violently. People stared in disbelief as a dirty white cloud arose from the mountain, billowed into a vast tree shape and blew towards the town. Everyone scattered in panic, under a hail of small pumice stones. Within minutes, the sky was as dark as night and pierced by jagged lightning. Volcanic ash slowly began to bury the town, and by the second day ash and poisonous gas descended in a thick, burning blizzard.

What is a volcano?

Magma often collects in the magma chamber. On the surface magma cools and hardens to produce lava. Volcanoes also blast out stones, hot gases and ash formed from fine bits of magma. Some volcanoes are merely cracks in the ground. Others such as Vesuvius itself, are built into massive cone shapes by layers of lava and ash from previous eruptions.

In an eruption, molten rock from the magma chamber forces its way up through the vents.

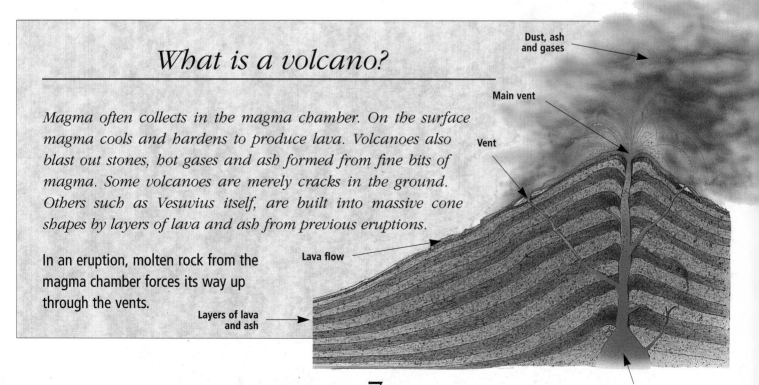

Dust, ash and gases

Main vent

Vent

Lava flow

Layers of lava and ash

Magma chamber

The most recent eruption of Vesuvius was in 1944. The huge cloud of ash that buried Pompeii in AD 79 may have looked like the one in this picture.

Inside Vesuvius

Just before the eruption, rising magma was trapped by a plug of hardened lava. The magma was under great pressure as more magma welled up from below. Gradually the plug broke up and the sudden drop in pressure allowed trapped gases in the magma to expand rapidly in a more or less continuous gas blast, hurling ash and debris over 20 km high. This type of catastrophe is now known as a Plinian eruption after Pliny the Younger, who first described it.

Escape from Vesuvius

A young man, named Pliny the Younger, and his mother had been staying at nearby Misenum. Pliny later described how the earth shook as they fled from their villa and headed for some nearby hills. They saw the waves of the sea crashing backwards and forwards, and '*... a black and dreadful cloud bursting out in gusts... [it] now and again yawned open to reveal long, fantastic flames, resembling flashes of lightning but much larger...*' Suddenly they were engulfed in a dark cloud of ash that reminded Pliny of being in a dark room.

When at last it grew light, Pliny and his mother returned to their villa. The countryside appeared smothered in ash, like a fall of grey snow. Pompeii had ceased to

Pliny and his family watch the eruption from their villa. Pliny's uncle died after trying to reach Pompeii to rescue some of his friends.

exist. Only the highest buildings showed above the sea of ash. More than 2,000 Pompeiians died in the catastrophe. Whole families suffocated, huddled together inside their houses. Roofs collapsed, crushing people beneath them. Thousands more may have died outside the town.

Frozen in time
Archaeologists began to uncover Pompeii in 1748, and the work continues today. The fall of ash has preserved many details of life in the town. We can even identify some of the victims, from the names found on their personal possessions.

Volcanic explosions from the crater of Stromboli throw rocks high into the air.

Other types of eruption

In addition to Plinian eruptions there are two other main types of eruption. In a Hawaiian eruption, runny lava spills from a crater and can travel great distances, destroying everything in its path. Eventually, layers of lava harden to form low, gently sloping shield volcanoes like those on Hawaii in the Pacific Ocean.

In a Strombolian eruption, the magma is less runny but is full of trapped gas. As the magma rises to the surface, this gas expands, causing explosions that throw magma fragments into the air. This rock debris accumulates around the vent to form steep-sided volcanoes, such as Stromboli in Italy.

Red hot lava glows through the crust of a Hawaiian lava flow. As it cools the crust hardens and eventually the entire lava flow will turn into solid rock.

The death of St Pierre

Visitors came to the town of St Pierre in Martinique to admire its old, white washed buildings, its bustling port and its wide bay full of sailing ships. In 1902, however St Pierre was completely wiped out in an eruption that was even more devastating than the catastrophe which destroyed Pompeii.

The volcano of Mount Pelée, 7 km to north, had been erupting for over a fortnight. On 2 May, a fine drizzle of ash descended on Le Prêcheur, a nearby town and, by the following day, the rooftops in St Pierre were buried under 5 cm of fine grey ash. As the ash fall continued, children were given a holiday from school.

The townspeople were divided – some decided to leave, but others claimed that the town was still safe. As conditions in the town continued to worsen, Mrs Prentiss, the wife of a US diplomat, wrote: *'The smell of sulphur [a gas produced by the volcano] is so strong that the horses in the street stop and snort, and*

The town of St Pierre is dominated by Mount Pelée, the volcano that destroyed it in 1902.

St Pierre before the eruption. When the volcano erupted, many of the ships in the bay were destroyed. One vessel, the *Rosaima* was set on fire by the blast, and only 20 of the 68 passengers and crew survived.

some of them drop in their harness and die of suffocation. Many of the people are obliged to wear wet handkerchiefs to protect themselves from the strong fumes of sulphur.'

On 5 May, the sides of a lake in the crater of Mount Pelée collapsed, causing a mud flow that destroyed a sugar factory. The following day lightning played around the summit of the volcano and the rain of ash continued. However, an election was due on 11 May and the authorities wanted to reassure the voters that they were in no danger. On 7 May the editor of *Les Colonies*, the local paper, began his main article by asking 'Where could one be better off than in St Pierre?' At about 7 am on 8 May, Fernand Clerc, a wealthy landowner, was alarmed to see the needle of his barometer moving violently due to rapid changes in air pressure. He bundled his wife and children into his carriage and drove out of town. Looking back, they saw a sheet of flame and what Clerc described as a 'great torrent of black fog' engulfing the town.

St Pierre after the eruption. The volcanic blast was followed by a terrible fire that reduced most of the ruins to ashes.

At 7.52 am, many of the inhabitants were eating their breakfast. In a small stone-built jail was 25-year-old Louis-Auguste Sylbaris who had been sentenced to eight days imprisonment in the stone dungeon. He was never to forget the moment when disaster struck: *'It was about eight... suddenly a tremendous noise burst out, everyone calling for help, cried out "I am burning! I am dying!" Five minutes later, there were no more cries, except mine.'*

Outside, the ruins of St Pierre were ablaze and nearly everyone else in the town was dead. The disaster had killed 30,000 people in less than three minutes.

A search party found Sylbaris three days later. He was still trapped in his dungeon, covered in burns and almost mad from thirst and terror.

The dungeon where Sylbaris was imprisoned. Its thick walls and sheltered position protected Sylbaris from the blast.

An avalanche of destruction

The blast that destroyed St Pierre was a 'nuée ardente' – a glowing avalanche of red – hot gases, pulverized magma and ash. The massive sideways blast was channelled by a ravine towards the town. It was witnessed by an officer aboard a passenger ship in St Pierre's harbour: 'There was no warning; the side of the volcano was ripped out and there hurled towards us a solid wall of flame. It sounded like a thousand cannons... The town vanished before our eyes.'

The town of Armero after it was buried by a volcanic mud-slide. The mud has destroyed or buried most of the houses. Many survivors took refuge on the roof-tops.

Torrent of mud

On 13 November 1985, as the rain poured down in the deserted streets of Armero, Colombia, a lone fireman frantically ran from house to house blowing a whistle. It was a last-minute warning of the tide of destruction that was roaring towards the town.

At 11.15 that night, Armero was hit by a *lahar* – a volcanic mud-flow. The mud was like warm, wet cement mixed with small stones. As the *lahar* passed, the stones stripped the bark from trees. In some places, the mud was 3.5 m deep and it sucked people down like quicksand. Within minutes of its arrival, more than 23,000 people lay entombed beneath Armero's shattered buildings.

This photograph shows a nuée ardente from Mount Pelée a few months after the destruction of St Pierre. The men who took this picture almost lost their lives. The cloud of red-hot ash was moving at 200 km/h and its temperature was about 700 °C.

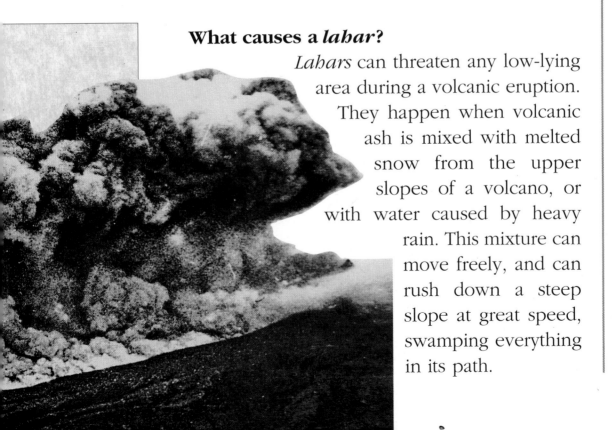

What causes a *lahar*?

Lahars can threaten any low-lying area during a volcanic eruption. They happen when volcanic ash is mixed with melted snow from the upper slopes of a volcano, or with water caused by heavy rain. This mixture can move freely, and can rush down a steep slope at great speed, swamping everything in its path.

'The world is ending!'

Sixteen-year-old Slaye Molina was at home with her family when the lahar *struck Armero in Colombia:* 'At 11.05, the lights went out. I held matches to see my watch. At 11.15, the mud came. Like a cloud. People screamed, "The world is ending!" We ran upstairs to our terrace, but we saw another house collapse, so we rushed outside...'

In the rain and darkness, Slaye and a friend followed a stampede of screaming people towards a nearby hill. Looking back, the young girl caught a glimpse of her uncle, grandmother and aunt embracing as if for the last time. Slaye and her friend were to spend three days marooned on the hill-top. When at last they escaped Slaye discovered that her uncle and grandfather had survived. They were all lucky to be alive.

In the wake of disaster

Major disasters, such as the destruction of Armero, are followed by a massive emergency relief operation. The first aim is to care for the injured and to search for survivors trapped in the wreckage of collapsed buildings. The homeless victims need blankets, tents, food, fuel and medical supplies – all of

A rescuer tries to help a victim buried in the volcanic mud of Armero.

Right A medical worker holds a baby rescued from the Armero mud-flow. Many of the survivors were suffering from shock and from the cold, and the baby has been wrapped in blankets to keep it warm.

Below This injured survivor from Armero has been heli-coptered to a nearby hospital.

which need to be transported to the disaster area. This can be extremely difficult and dangerous if the disaster has occurred in a remote location.

WHICH ERUPTIONS HAVE BEEN MOST DESTRUCTIVE?

THE Krakatoa group of islands lie in the Sunda Strait, between the larger islands of Java and Sumatra, in an area that suffers from more volcanic activity than most places on earth. The original group consisted of several islands which had been formed by three volcanoes – Perbuwatan, Danan and Krakatoa itself, the largest of the three. In 1883, there had not been any eruptions for many years, and the islands were all overgrown with dense, tropical vegetation.

The region was shaken by a series of earthquakes, starting in the 1870s, but in May 1883 sudden eruptions blasted ash and steam 10 km into the air. The explosions died away, but

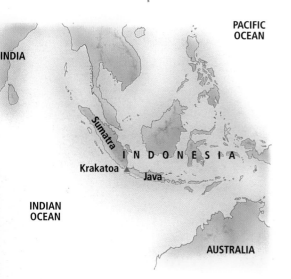

Above Krakatoa and its neighbouring islands.

Krakatoa before it exploded on 27 August 1883. Hundreds of people lived on the island. They made a living by growing rice or fishing in the sea. Although the island looks quite peaceful, the smoking mountain is an ominous warning of the future.

in the following months there were more. They grew in strength, and by mid-August 1883 Danan and Perbuwatan were exploding every few minutes.

Then, between 23 and 28 August, the sleeping giant Krakatoa burst into life erupting in an almost continuous series of huge explosions, each merging into the next, to make a sound like constant, deafening thunder.

Left The explosion of Krakatoa. The cloud of ash blew 80 km into the air and covered a vast area. Ships found floating debris from the eruption 500 km away.

Why did Krakatoa erupt?

The violent explosions were probably caused by large nuées ardentes entering the surrounding sea and blowing up. Danan, Perbuwatan and part of Krakatoa collapsed into the magma chamber as it emptied, and eventually formed a vast crater called a caldera. In 1927, a new volcano appeared and was named Anak Krakatoa, meaning 'child of Krakatoa'.

Above right The smoking crater of Anak Krakatoa. Since 1927 the volcano has grown bit by bit due to frequent eruptions.

Right The islands before the eruption (**1**), the remains of Krakatoa after the eruption (**2**), and Anak Krakatoa, (**3**).

Over 40,500 million cubic metres of rock disintegrated in the eruption. The immense volcanic activity created huge tsunami – some up to 50 m high – which swept across the low-lying coasts of Java and Sumatra. Over 300 towns and villages were flooded, and many thousands of people drowned.

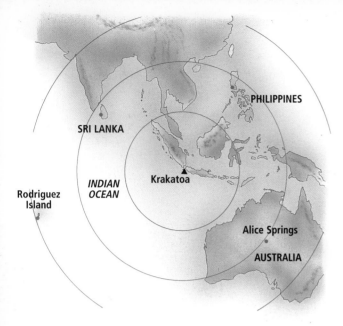

The map shows the huge area in which people heard the sound of the Krakatoa explosion.

The biggest bang

The Krakatoa eruption was the loudest explosion in human history. It was heard at Rodriguez Island, 4,772 km away on the other side of the Indian Ocean, and it shocked people in Australia, 3,250 km away. It was followed by another huge tsunami which swept away many people who had returned to the wreckage of their homes. As the giant waves travelled across the world's oceans, they sank river boats in India and caused unusually high tides on the British coast. Up to 36,000 people were dead. Many had been drowned by the tsunami or killed by the diseases that infected the starving survivors.

Dangerous waters

On the morning of 27 August, a passing ship, the Loudon, *was almost swamped by several giant waves 80 km north of Krakatoa. The sky turned black with falling ash and the ship was pounded by powerful winds and struck by lightning. By the time daylight returned the following morning the ship's decks were covered in 18 cm of ash.*

The crew of the Charles Bal *off the coast of Java heard:* 'A fearful explosion in the direction of Krakatoa... [Within 15 minutes] we were enclosed in a darkness that might also be felt. We had to grope about on deck, and although speaking to one another, could not see each other.'

A giant wave swept the Dutch warship *Berouw* 2 km inland.

Fire Mountain

People who live near the peaceful, beautiful peak of Mount St Helens, in Washington State, USA, call it 'Fire Mountain', the name given to it by Native Americans. Mount St Helens had erupted five times in the previous 280 years, throwing out clouds of ash and fire.

On 27 March 1980, Mount St Helens had begun to belch out huge clouds of steam and ash. Everyone was evacuated, except 84-year-old Harry Truman, the owner of Mount St Helens Lodge, 6 km north of the volcano. He told reporters, *'If the mountain goes, I'm going to stay right here. I stuck it out for 54 years and I can stick it out now.'*

In the following month, it became clear that something even more alarming was happening. The north face of the mountain was bulging like a huge blister around an area called 'Goat Rock'. It was being forced outwards by the increasing pressure of the magma underneath.

Sunday 18 May dawned bright and clear. A pair of sightseers set up a camera on a neighbouring mountain to take pictures of the eruption.

The vast ash cloud blasting from Mount St Helens engulfs a forest and a mobile home. Over 500 sq km of forests were flattened by the eruption.

In the devastated area around the volcano, the forests were smashed to matchwood. Everything was covered in grey volcanic ash. But this ash proved fertile for growing plants. Today the area is once again covered in trees and flowers.

At 8.32 am, the north face of Mount St Helens seemed to slip as the shock of earthquakes broke the bulge loose. An avalanche of 8,000 million tonnes of ice, rock and mud thundered down the slope, followed by a huge Plinian eruption of grey ash and gas. After snapping a few hasty pictures, the photographers ran for their lives.

The eruption changed the shape of Mount St Helens, blowing 400 m off the top of the mountain and leaving a crater 1.5 km wide.

'This is it!...'

From his observation post 10 km northwest of the volcano, a young scientist, Dr David Johnston, also saw the blast. As the huge cloud of burning debris tore down on him, he rushed to his radio and called his base at Vancouver, Washington. 'Vancouver, Vancouver, this is it!' he shouted. Then the radio went dead. Harry Truman and David Johnston were among the 57 victims of the eruption. Their bodies were never recovered.

Left The cloud of ash from Mount St Helens towers above the city of Portland, Oregon. Ash from the volcano fell from the sky and blocked roads hundreds of kilometres away.

Before

After

Within minutes, an area 30 km wide had been destroyed. Rivers had become torrents of volcanic mud, forests were flattened or burning and a billowing mass of dust and ash rose 25 km into the sky. The eruption continued for four days; every second, Mount St Helens blasted out enough destructive power to flatten a small city.

Traces of destruction

The Earth has been scarred by far greater eruptions than Krakatoa or Mount St Helens. For example, Lake Toba in Sumatra lies in a caldera 100 km long and 30 km wide which was formed by an eruption 73,500 years ago. The eruption ejected about 2,700 times more ash than Mount St Helens. Many scientists believe that such huge eruptions can make the weather cooler because the vast clouds of ash float high into the atmosphere and block out the sunlight.

Lake Toba, Sumatra. This peaceful lake was once the scene of a violent volcanic eruption.

WHAT HAPPENS IN AN EARTHQUAKE?

Above In 1758, a terrible earthquake struck Lisbon, Portugal. Buildings toppled like cards and fires broke out. A tsunami swept in from the sea and drowned many people. About 60,000 people were killed in the disaster.

OF all the sudden natural disasters that strike our world, earthquakes are, so far, the most dangerous. A single large 'quake can cause enormous amounts of destruction and huge loss of life. One such earthquake, which rocked Shanxi in China on 2 February 1556, is thought to have killed 830,000 people – nine times as many as the worst volcanic eruption.

A modern-day 'quake
History is full of disastrous earthquakes. But even today, in a city of well-constructed buildings and trained emergency rescue services, an earthquake can cause massive devastation.

On 17 October 1989 San Francisco, USA was struck by an earthquake that destroyed over 1,400 homes. This man was one of many people who fled the area taking only what they could carry.

Why do earthquakes happen?

The plates of solid rock that make up the Earth's surface float on a mass of hot, plastic rock below them. They are all moving in different directions, at the rate of a few millimetres a year. In some places the huge plates grind slowly past each other; elsewhere, one plate is forced underneath another.

Sometimes, two plates don't slide past each other smoothly and they get stuck. When this happens, enormous pressures build up. Eventually, these pressures become so great that something has to give. The plates then free themselves suddenly with a huge jolt, which causes strong

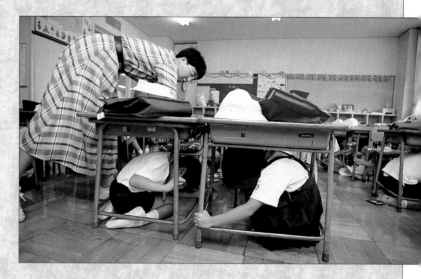

Above School children in Japan are taught to shelter under their desks during an earthquake. The desks will help to protect the children from falling objects.

shock waves to spread out through the Earth in all directions. When these shock waves reach the surface, they can cause earthquakes. Fortunately, earthquakes tend to occur at the edges of the plates, most of which are under the sea. So most places on land are safe.

When an earthquake happens, shock waves spread out from the focus at a speed of several kilometres a second.

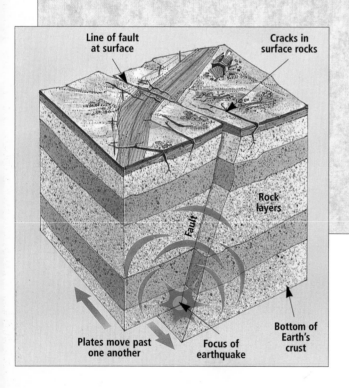

Line of fault at surface

Cracks in surface rocks

Rock layers

Fault

Plates move past one another

Focus of earthquake

Bottom of Earth's crust

At 5.04 pm on 17 October 1989, 62,000 baseball fans were packed into Candlestick Park in San Francisco, USA. They were eagerly awaiting the start of the World Series game between the Oakland Athletics and the San Francisco Giants.

In the clean-up after the San Francisco earthquake, wrecked cars and other debris was piled up in the streets.

Measuring earthquakes

Every year there about 500,000 earthquakes, of which only about 1,000 are powerful enough to cause serious damage. Earthquake vibrations spread out in all directions like ripples on a pond, but they are felt most strongly around the point called the epicentre directly above the place where the jolt occurred – the focus.

The energy produced by an earthquake is recorded on an instrument called a seismometer and is measured using the Richter Scale. A shock that measures 7 on the Richter Scale is a major earthquake. The actual effects of an earthquake on buildings and people are measured using the Modified Mercalli Scale.

A seismogramme for the San Francisco earthquake of 17 October 1989. The sharp zig-zags were made as the earthquake shook the seismograph's pen.

The 12 levels of the Modified Mercalli Scale. An earthquake at level 1 is hardly felt, while at level 12 there is total destruction.

In other parts of the city, people were going about their normal daily business. Thousands of commuters were driving home from work along Highway 880 and the other elevated, double-decker roads that criss-cross San Francisco. In the suburb of Menlo Park, just south of the city, Father Kevin Doheny, a Catholic priest on a visit from Ireland, had just left the home of his American host: *'The house began to rock. First of all there was a dreadful rumbling noise. It was frightening. My friend, Danny, said, "Let's get out of here." We ran out and saw the [swimming] pool overflowing on the lawn, like a rough sea…'*

Back at Candlestick Park, there was total pandemonium. As the stadium shook, all the players ran on to the pitch, hoping to be safe from falling masonry. Many of the spectators were terrified, and a man who had climbed one of the tall floodlights hung on for dear life as the huge steel structure rocked and swayed beneath him. A 15-cm crack opened beneath one massive section of seating. Incredibly, no one was killed.

Elsewhere in the city, buildings and bridges collapsed, water pipes fractured and roads were cracked wide open. In the Marina area, massive fires raged out of control. Worst of all, the upper section of Highway 880 had collapsed, crushing many cars on the lower section.

The San Andreas Fault

Earthquakes occur along deep cracks called faults. These are formed when rocks break apart under the pressure of plate movement. The San Francisco earthquake was caused by movement along the San Andreas Fault – which is, in fact, a complex series of faults caused by the Pacific Ocean plate and the American continental plate grinding past one another in opposite directions. In 1906, the San Andreas Fault suddenly moved 3 m, and the resulting earthquake destroyed San Francisco and killed 452 people.

USA

Sacramento

San Francisco

Las Vegas

San Andreas Fault

Santa Barbara

Los Angeles

PACIFIC
OCEAN

San Diego

MEXICO

Above The San Andreas Fault stretches 1,125 km through the state of California, USA.

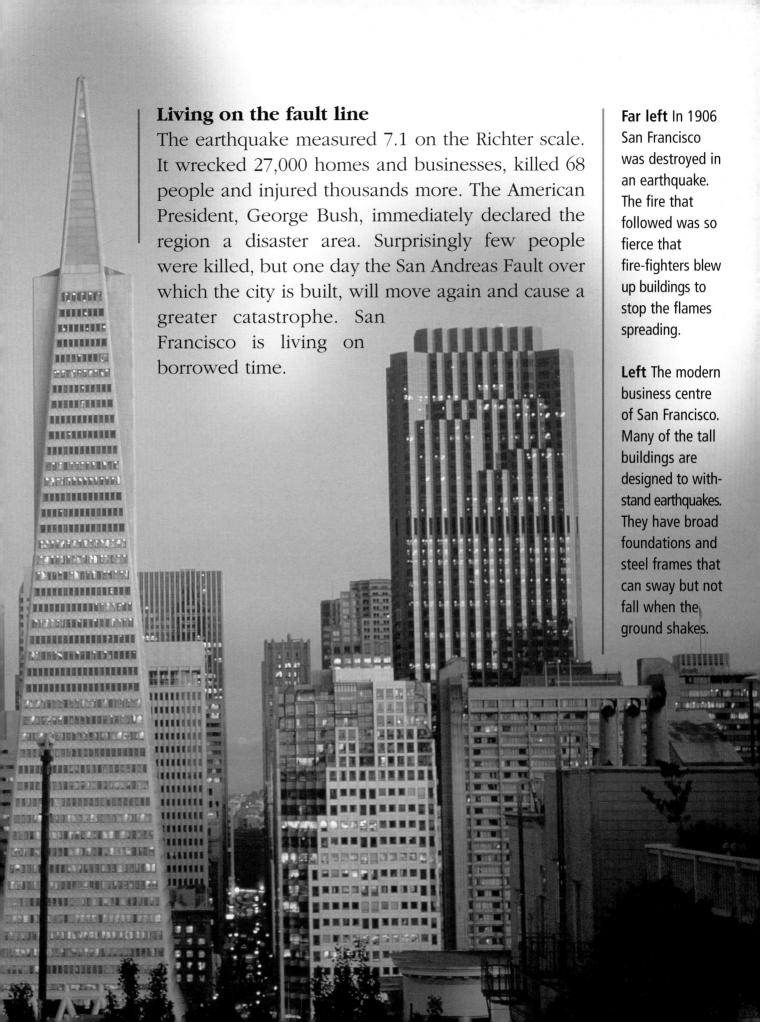

Living on the fault line

The earthquake measured 7.1 on the Richter scale. It wrecked 27,000 homes and businesses, killed 68 people and injured thousands more. The American President, George Bush, immediately declared the region a disaster area. Surprisingly few people were killed, but one day the San Andreas Fault over which the city is built, will move again and cause a greater catastrophe. San Francisco is living on borrowed time.

Far left In 1906 San Francisco was destroyed in an earthquake. The fire that followed was so fierce that fire-fighters blew up buildings to stop the flames spreading.

Left The modern business centre of San Francisco. Many of the tall buildings are designed to with-stand earthquakes. They have broad foundations and steel frames that can sway but not fall when the ground shakes.

DO EARTHQUAKES CAUSE OTHER DISASTERS?

AT 3.20 pm on 31 May, the streets of Yungay, Peru were deserted while the villagers watched the 1970 World Cup on television. Suddenly, the ground shook and several houses collapsed. It was an earthquake registering 7.7 on the Richter Scale.

High on the nearby mountain of Nevado de Huascaran, the shock triggered a huge fall of ice and rock. As it roared down the mountain at 400 km/h, the avalanche scooped up loose rocks from the steep slopes, and swelled into an 80-m-high wave of rocks and mud. Huge boulders – some weighing as much as 100 tonnes – were swept along like pebbles. The village of Ranrahirca, directly in its path, was smashed to pieces. Part of the avalanche surged over a 250-m-high ridge… and fell on Yungay.

An avalanche happens when a mass of snow and ice slips down a mountainside.

Yungay and the Andes Mountains of Peru. In 1970 this area was hit by a powerful earthquake.

As the earthquake had struck, many villagers had run out of their homes, only to see the avalanche hurtling down the mountain towards them. Hundreds of panic-stricken people ran towards the cemetery hill – the only patch of land higher than the oncoming wave of rock and mud. They had just three minutes before the landslide struck. There were about 20,000 people in Yungay that day, but few of them survived.

Yungay had been a beautiful old village with a wide square and its own cathedral. After the landslide there was nothing left but a few scattered ruins and a desert of boulders.

These children were lucky to survive the disaster that destroyed Yungay. After the earthquake, the homeless survivors suffered from cold and the freezing rain.

Escape from the avalanche

Señor Casaverde, one of the survivors, later reported how he ran for the cemetery hill: 'I reached the upper part of the hill just in time, as the debris avalanche hit the lower slopes. My friends and I must have saved ourselves by only ten seconds. Lower down the hill, I saw a man carrying two children who, as the wave [of rocks] hit him, threw the children to safety. Both the man and two women near him were swept away.'

Tsunami!

Just as earthquakes on land can cause landslides, earthquakes under the sea can trigger giant waves, known as tsunami. These waves have killed thousands of people, mainly in countries bordering the Pacific Ocean.

On 8 August 1868, one such wave struck the coastal town of Arica in Chile. Several ships were lying at anchor in the calm, blue waters of Iquique Bay. Among them was USS *Wateree*, a two-masted American warship. At about 4 pm, Lieutenant L.G. Billings was talking to his captain, when the ship seemed to shudder.

The two men rushed on to the deck. As they looked on, Arica was devastated by an earthquake. A boatload of rescuers set out from the *Wateree*, but they were all drowned by a violent surge of the sea. Then the water suddenly withdrew, stranding

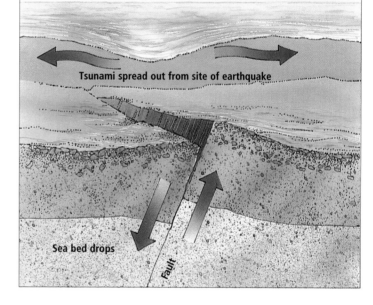

Tsunami spread out from site of earthquake

Sea bed drops

Fault

Above In an undersea earthquake, part of the sea bed drops. Water rushes into the gap and, when it is full, the water washes back in the opposite direction. This causes massive waves called tsunami.

thousands of fish and grounding every vessel in the bay. The water then returned again in another massive surge that wrecked many of the ships.

A ship hit by a tsunami. Like the *Wateree* this vessel had no chance to escape.

Several hours later a lookout spotted the foaming crest and massive, dark shape of a tsunami. Lieutenant Billings later described the horror of that moment: *'We were chained to the bed of the sea, powerless to escape… we could do nothing but watch this monstrous wave… We could only hold on to the rails and wait for the catastrophe.'*

Below The town of Anchorage, Alaska, USA after a tsunami struck in 1964. The massive wave has washed these boats high up on the hillside.

A tsunami hits Hilo pier on the Pacific island of Hawaii. The man arrowed (bottom right) was killed by this massive wave.

With a terrible crash, the wave swamped the *Wateree*. After a seemingly endless wait, the ship resurfaced, with water pouring from her decks and her gasping crew still clutching the rails. As dawn broke they saw that the *Wateree* and two other ships had been swept three km inland by the huge power of the tsunami. Nothing remained of Arica but a heap of debris.

Inside the tsunami

Tsunami are caused by the sudden movement of the sea bed during an earthquake. At sea a tsunami is only slightly higher than an average wave, but as it moves into shallow water near the coast it slows down and becomes much higher – up to 50 m.

WHEN A HURRICANE STRIKES

A hurricane strikes the coast of Florida, USA. This area is frequently hit by hurricanes blowing in from the Caribbean Sea.

HURRICANES are immense, spinning masses of air which form over the world's warm oceans, near the Equator. They can measure more than 2,000 km across and are the most destructive weather systems on Earth.

At the centre of a hurricane is an area called the eye, about 15 km across. Although the eye is quite calm, fierce winds rage around it at up to 300 km/h, tearing up trees, cars and even houses.

Hurricanes don't stay in one place, but are pushed along by the prevailing winds at between 15 and 40 km/h. As a result, they often move towards the land, where they can cause great damage to coastal regions.

A helicopter lifts a hurricane survivor to safety. This particular hurricane in 1965 wrecked homes and flooded part of the coast in Louisiana, USA.

Inside a hurricane

A hurricane forms when warm, moist air rises above the sea to form massive clouds, between 10 and 15 km high. Cold air rushes in from below to replace the rising air and it, too, is drawn upwards.

Right Winds swirling around the central eye of a hurricane. Most hurricanes develop in the summer and autumn when the seas are warm, and they generally last about 9 days.

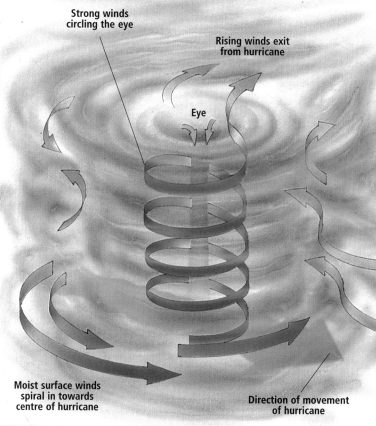

Strong winds circling the eye

Rising winds exit from hurricane

Eye

Moist surface winds spiral in towards centre of hurricane

Direction of movement of hurricane

The hurricane spins as a result of the Coriolis force, which is caused by the spinning of the Earth in space. Because of this rotation, winds and ocean currents do not move across the Earth in straight lines but are deflected to the right in the Southern Hemisphere and to the left in the Northern Hemisphere. This is why a hurricane spins — and why the water spins down the plughole when you pull out the plug after a bath.

Left This damage was caused by a hurricane that swept across southern Florida, USA, in 1992.

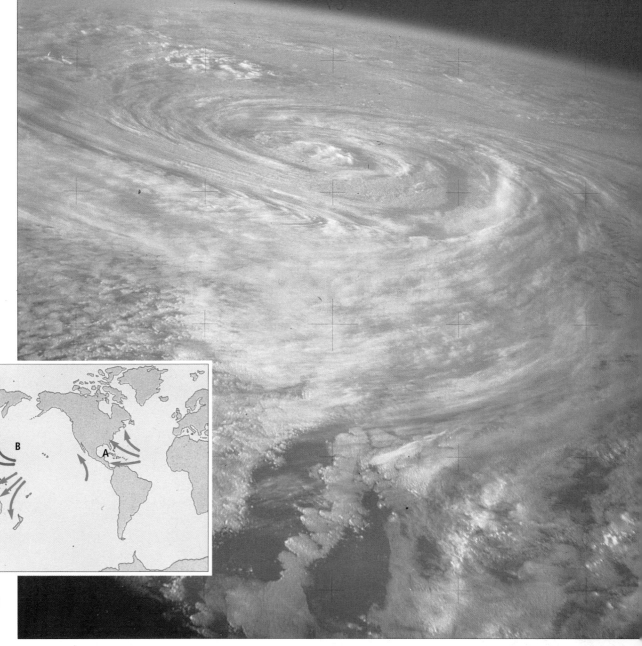

Right A hurricane seen from space. The whirling clouds are about 10 km thick and several hundred kilometres across.

Above The areas of the world where hurricanes (**A**), typhoons (**B**) and cyclones (**C**) occur. In Australia, these storms are sometimes called 'Willy-willies' (**D**).

Hurricanes occur in the Atlantic Ocean. Similar storms in the Indian Ocean and the Bay of Bengal are called cyclones, while those in the western North Pacific are known as typhoons. Each year, these powerful storms are named in alphabetical order as they appear. The first is given a name beginning with A, the second, B, and so on.

Damage caused by Cyclone Tracy in Darwin, Australia. The powerful wind has torn this house to pieces. The cyclone destroyed 90 per cent of the buildings in the city and made 9,000 people homeless.

Cyclone Tracy

The city of Darwin, Australia, was hit by a cyclone on Christmas Day 1974. Many of the inhabitants were relaxing at home, sleeping off their dinner or opening presents. None could have imagined that, by the end of the day, many of them would be sifting through the wreckage of their homes.

During the morning, the clouds above Darwin thickened and a howling wind grew up. Many people were too busy with their Christmas celebrations to listen to the warnings about the approach of Cyclone Tracy, which were broadcast on both radio and TV.

When the cyclone hit, the first thoughts of Roslyn Wise were for the safety of her children: *'During the storm my husband and I huddled under two beds pushed together. We sang songs and did everything we could think of to keep the children from being frightened.'* All of the bedrooms in their house were wrecked – except for the one in which the family were sheltering.

In the suburb of Nightcliffe, Mrs Norma Walker watched in horror as her car somersaulted in a whirling wind full of flying debris. The cyclone destroyed her house. For some days afterwards, she and her homeless neighbours cooked their food on barbecues in the open air. She said that at first people were too shocked to clear up or even to talk. Later, however, they set up groups to care for the injured. Many people thought only of getting away. There were long queues for tickets at the airport and the bus station.

A cyclone in Bangladesh

The hurricane that hit Darwin in 1974 caused an

enormous amount of damage to buildings, but few people lost their lives. On 30 April 1991, a cyclone struck the densely populated coastal area of Bangladesh, and the loss of life was much worse. One of the survivors, Rashim Sarkar, lived with his wife and three children on an island at the mouth of the Ganges River. Their home was a hut made of bamboo and straw built on a mud platform in the village of Bainchang.

The islands of Bangladesh are threatened by cyclones because they are low and flat. When a cyclone makes the sea rise, these houses will be flooded or swept away.

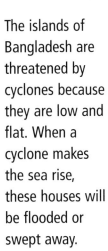

Many people who live by the sea are in danger from cyclones. The picture shows a cyclone wrecking the houseboat of a Chinese family in Hong Kong in 1906.

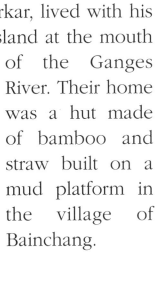

This settlement in Bangladesh was wrecked by floods following the 1991 cyclone. The buffalo in the fields were drowned by the floodwaters.

Rashim had once been a rice farmer on the mainland, but was forced to leave his land because he could not afford the rent. Although Rashim knew about the danger of tidal surges caused by cyclones, he stayed on the island because the fertile soil of the islands was easy to farm – and because he had nowhere else to go.

The people of the island had no televisions and few radios, so they did not hear the cyclone warnings broadcast on 30 April. The first hint of danger came when some fishermen told the village headman that they had seen big storm clouds in the bay.

What is a tornado?

Tornadoes are rather like hurricanes except they form over the land instead of the sea. A tornado develops when a column of rising warm air starts to spin inside a thundercloud. This spinning air sucks more air from below as it gets bigger and faster. Despite their power, few tornadoes are more than a few hundred metres across. At ground level, tornadoes behave like uncontrollable vacuum cleaners, sucking debris from the ground and whirling it high in the air. Sometimes they change direction for no apparent reason. The types of destruction they cause can be equally unpredictable: sometimes they lift entire houses from their foundations, at others they tear the feathers from birds without harming them.

Although tornadoes can strike anywhere, they are most frequent in Australia and central parts of the USA. One area of the USA, from Nebraska to Texas, is nicknamed 'tornado alley' because it is hit so frequently. Although hundreds of minor tornadoes are reported in the USA each year, it is the few large ones that kill most people.

Above This tornado in the USA has come down to earth from the thundercloud above it.

This map shows the states of the USA where tornadoes are most common.

Right A tornado speeds towards a small Australian town in 1939. Tornadoes can move at up to 120 km/h – much faster than people who are trying to run away.

Victims of flooding in Bangladesh carry their belongings to safety.

As the clouds darkened and the wind grew stronger, the villagers huddled round the small radio in the headman's hut, anxious for news. Then the first rain began to fall.

The hurricane battered the coast for seven hours, and the heavy rain it brought caused flooding in many parts of the mainland. On the islands the situation was far worse. Twelve islands had been hit by massive surges from the sea; twelve others were still completely under water. Two thousand villages had been wrecked. Bainchang was one of them.

Rashim's grief

Hours later, Rashim sat in the ruins of his home, too distressed even to eat the food he was offered. He told news reporters how he had held on to his wife and their children as the storm whirled around them. Then, as the eye of the hurricane passed overhead, the waves had suddenly increased in size. A huge wave had swept over Rashim's hut, tearing his family from his grasp.

Every hut in the village had been smashed and 65 people were feared drowned.

A victim of the 1991 cyclone stands in front of the wreckage of his home. He and his son are lucky to be alive.

This photograph of a hurricane was taken from space. It has been coloured to show the strength of the winds. Those in the red area are strongest, then the orange. The eye is in the centre. Such pictures can help scientists to tell where hurricanes will strike.

Throughout the islands, at least 50,000 people were killed. However, even this was not the worst disaster to have hit the coast of Bangladesh. On 12 and 13 November 1970, over 500,000 people – and possibly up to a million – are thought to have been killed when a cyclone swept across the islands at the mouth of the Ganges.

We can't stop hurricanes happening, any more than we can prevent other natural disasters. The best we can do is try to predict when and where the disasters will happen and prepare for the worst. Despite all our efforts, however, volcanic eruptions, earthquakes and hurricanes will continue to cause devastation and loss of life.

Right Waves crash against a beach as a hurricane comes ashore. This is a dangerous time for any people living nearby.

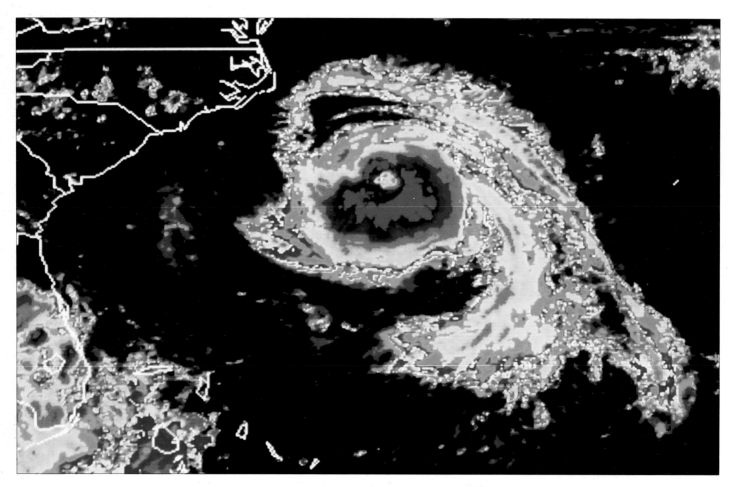

The storm surge

The fast-moving air of a hurricane presses down on the sea, but in the calmer eye this pressure is less and the sea bulges upwards. As the eye of the hurricane comes ashore, the water in the bulge piles up, forming a massive tide that spreads out and swamps low-lying areas. This tide is even higher if the wind is also blowing towards the shore. Storm surges have hit Bangladesh 57 times in 180 years.

Timeline

AD **1900**   **1940**   **1980**

AD 79

Eruption of Vesuvius destroys Pompeii and neighbouring town of Herculaneum

1556

Earthquake kills 830,000 people in Shanxi province, China

1755

Earthquake and tsunami devastate Lisbon, Portugal, and kill 60,000 people

1815

Eruption of Tambora, in what is now Indonesia, kills 90,000 people

1883

Eruption of Mount Krakatoa in Sunda Strait off Java

1902

Eruption of Mount Pelée destroys St Pierre, Martinique

1906

San Francisco, USA, destroyed by earthquake

1920

200,000 people killed by earthquake in Kansu, China

1923

Tokyo and Yokohama, Japan, destroyed by earthquake, killing 123,000 people

1925

823 people killed by tornado in Annapolis, USA

1970

Earthquake triggers landslide that destroys Yungay, Peru

1974

Tornado shatters town of Xenia, USA. Spate of tornadoes sweeps North America. Cyclone Tracy devastates Darwin, Australia

1979

Hurricane David kills 4,000 people in Puerto Rico and southeastern USA

1980

Eruption of Mount St Helens, USA

1985

Armero, Colombia, flattened by volcanic mud-slide

1986

1,742 killed by poisonous gas from volcano in Cameroon, Africa

1989

Earthquake strikes San Francisco, USA

1991

Cyclone hits Bangladesh. Storm surges kill thousands of people

1995

Kobe, Japan, devastated by earthquake

GLOSSARY

Ash The small pieces of magma, less than 2 mm wide, which are blasted from a volcano.

Caldera A very large crater, shaped like a wide bowl. It is formed when the summit of a volcano collapses into the magma chamber during a big eruption. Calderas are often filled by lakes.

Fault A line along which rocks have split apart due to movements of the Earth's plates.

Hurricane A huge, whirling storm in which the winds travel at up to 300 km/h.

Lahar A volcanic mudflow, formed when hot ash mixes with water from melted ice or heavy rain. The wet, slippery mud flows down the steep slopes of the volcano.

Lava Molten rock which pours on to the surface of the Earth during a volcanic eruption. It is still called lava when it hardens.

Magma Rock which is molten beneath the Earth's surface.

Magma chamber The area beneath a volcano where magma collects before an eruption.

Molten Something which has become so hot it has melted.

Nuée ardente The glowing avalanche of red-hot gases and ash that pours down the slopes of certain volcanoes during an eruption.

Plates The huge slabs of rock, often thousands of kilometres wide, that make up the Earth's surface layer, or crust.

Storm surge A massive burst of sea water often caused as the eye of a hurricane comes ashore. This is even bigger when the wind is blowing off the sea.

Tsunami A colossal wave caused by an undersea earthquake. In the open sea, a tsunami can travel at speeds of 800 km/h.

FURTHER INFORMATION

BOOKS

Earthquakes and Volcanoes by Basil Booth (Cloverleaf, 'Repairing the Damage' series, 1992)

Hurricanes and Typhoons by Jacqueline Dineen (Gloucester Press, 'Natural Disasters' series, 1991)

Volcanic Eruptions by Jacqueline Dineen (Gloucester Press, 'Natural Disasters' series, 1991)

Earthquake by John Dudman (Wayland, 'The Violent Earth' series, 1992)

Volcano by John Dudman (Wayland, 'The Violent Earth' series, 1992)

FILMS AND VIDEOS

Earthquake! (CIC Video) About the destruction of Los Angeles in a fictional earthquake.

In the Shadow of Vesuvius (National Geographic Video). A film about the destruction of Pompeii in AD 79.

CD-ROM

The Violent Earth by Sally Morgan (Wayland, 1995)

INDEX